Twenty to Make
Leather
Jewellery

Natalia Colman

Search Press

First published in 2015

Search Press Limited
Wellwood, North Farm Road,
Tunbridge Wells, Kent TN2 3DR

Text copyright © Natalia Colman 2015

Photographs by Fiona Murray on location
and Paul Bricknell at Search Press Studios

Photographs and design copyright
© Search Press Ltd 2015

All rights reserved. No part of this book, text,
photographs or illustrations may be reproduced
or transmitted in any form or by any means
by print, photoprint, microfilm, microfiche,
photocopier, internet or in any way known or
as yet unknown, or stored in a retrieval system,
without written permission obtained
beforehand from Search Press.

Print ISBN: 978-1-78221-199-0
ebook ISBN: 978-1-78126-258-0

The Publishers and author can accept no
responsibility for any consequences arising from
the information, advice or instructions given in
this publication.

Readers are permitted to reproduce any of the
items in this book for their personal use, or for
the purposes of selling for charity, free of charge
and without the prior permission of the Publishers.
Any use of the items for commercial purposes is
not permitted without the prior permission of
the Publishers.

Suppliers
If you have difficulty in obtaining any of the
materials and equipment mentioned in this book,
then please visit the Search Press website for
details of suppliers: www.searchpress.com

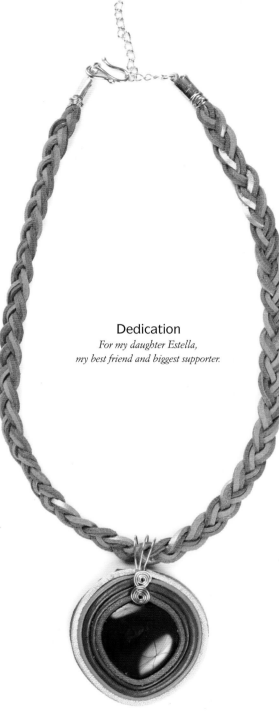

Dedication
For my daughter Estella,
my best friend and biggest supporter.

Printed in China

Contents

Introduction

Leather is traditionally used as a material for making handbags, gloves, shoes and accessories. I was fascinated by the idea of experimenting with different varieties of leather to see how I could turn it into jewellery.

Most of the jewellery in this book uses very small amounts of leather and simple tools, making it a very cost-effective craft. It is quite easy to find offcuts of leather in lots of different colours. You can find some unloved leather garments or bags in charity shops or even in your own wardrobe that can be upcycled into fabulous pieces of jewellery. All of the projects in this book are created quickly and easily using leather glue, wire or simple jewellery findings; no sewing or technical abilities are needed.

Leather is not only beautiful to look at and lovely to work with; it is also a medium that helps you make some stunning pieces of jewellery. I have designed a wide range of different projects and I hope you get as much enjoyment out of making and wearing them as I did creating them.

Tools and materials

Essential Tools

Leather scissors (1) are great for cutting out pieces of leather. They are particularly good for cutting specific shapes and for thin leathers up to 1.5mm ($^1/_{16}$in). **Spring tension shears (2)** are more heavy duty scissors for cutting leathers that are 1.5mm ($^1/_{16}$in) and thicker.

An **awl** is useful for marking points on leather and for making holes. It is a very sharp tool so always replace the safety cap when not in use.

An A3-sized **self-healing cutting mat** is the essential base to work on. Choose one with grid lines and measurements – a useful guide when creating patterns and cutting pieces of leather.

Choose a **steel ruler (3)** with cork backing so that it does not slip on smooth or shiny leather.

Keep **paintbrushes** in varying sizes for applying glue and decorative paint effects to leather.

Baby wipes are useful to have on hand to wipe away excess glue and for cleaning your tools.

Bulldog clips are used to hold glued pieces of leather in place while they dry.

A **rotary hole punch (4)**, which cuts a variety of hole sizes, is essential for cutting out perfect holes in leather. Twist the wheel in a counterclockwise direction to select the size.

Stamping tools (5) are useful for making decorative markings on leather.

Large **snap fasteners (6)** and **Sam Browne studs (7)** are useful fasteners for leather jewellery.

A **bone folder** is essential for smoothing the edges of vegetable tan leather and for making creases in fashion leather.

Types of leather

There are many different types of leather available. For some of the projects I have used **fashion leathers**; these are soft, colourful leathers, such as lamb nappa and pig suede leather, that are up to 1.5mm (1/16in) thick. I have also used **vegetable tan leather (8)** (also referred to as **tooling leather**). This is sturdier, comes in a variety of thicknesses and can be dyed, painted and stamped.

Jewellery items

Various jewellery-making tools and materials will also be needed. A **ring mandrel** is a tool for measuring your ring size. **Beading wire** is used to thread beads onto, and this is cut with **wire cutters**. **Flat-nosed pliers** are used for opening and closing jump rings (see right). **Round-nosed pliers** are used for making loops in wire. Jewellery findings such as **earwires**, **chains**, **jump rings**, **clasps**, **beads**, **faux pearls**, **gemstones** and **crimp beads** are also useful and widely available online and in craft stores.

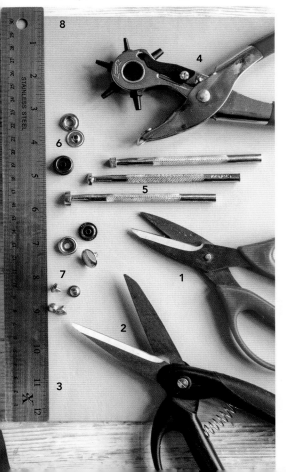

Techniques

Creating a pattern

1 Once you have planned your design, draw your pattern onto some card and cut it out. Check that the design is the right size and shape and has the right 'movement' before cutting any leather. You want to avoid making expensive mistakes, so take your time.

2 Place the card pattern on the underside of the leather and draw round it carefully with a ballpoint pen.

3 Cut out your leather shape(s). If you will be able to see both sides of the finished piece, make sure you cut inside the line you have drawn so that the pen marks cannot be seen.

4 Label your patterns and templates before storing them so that you can use them again for future projects.

Wet-forming leather

Leather can be given a whole different look by wetting it, forming it into shapes and drying it. If you are unsure about the effect this will have on a particular piece of leather you want to use, try this technique on a small test piece first.

1 Cut out the pieces of leather for your design.

2 Place them in a bowl of hand-hot water and allow the water to saturate the leather.

3 Remove the leather pieces from the water and pat them dry with a paper towel or cloth.

4 Form the pieces into the shape you want by moulding and twisting them. For petal shapes, it is a good idea to place these inside a small cup or jar to help them form a rounded shape.

5 Allow the pieces to dry at room temperature. You can speed the process up by placing them in a cool oven at 80°C/176°F/gas mark ¼.

6 After the pieces have dried, you can create your jewellery.

How to open and close a jump ring

1 Use two pairs of flat-nosed pliers to grip the jump ring on either side of the gap. Move one side towards you and the other away from you to open the jump ring. Do not pull the ring apart because it may distort the shape.

2 Once you have opened the jump ring, you can insert an earring wire, chain, clasp or an additional jump ring.

3 To close the jump ring, grip both ends with your pliers. Bend them back together again, wiggling the ends back and forth until you feel them sliding against one another. Your jump ring ends should be perfectly aligned when closed.

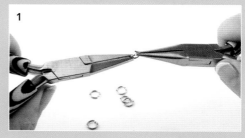

1

2

3

Feather Necklace & Earrings

Materials:

Sheet of card

10 x 15cm (4 x 6in) piece
of red nappa leather

Silver or gold fabric paint

40cm (15¾in) strand of beads

2 x 9mm (³⁄₈in) silver jump rings

2 x silver crimps and crimp covers

1m (39½in) length of beading wire

1 x toggle clasp

2 x 6mm (¼in) gold-coloured
jump rings

2 x earring wires

Tools:

Ballpoint pen

Piece of card

Leather scissors

Rotary hole punch

2 x flat-nosed pliers

Wire cutters

Small paintbrush

Instructions:

1 Draw a feather shape onto a piece of card and cut it out. Draw around the card template on the back of the leather with a ballpoint pen.

2 Cut out the feather shape, then cut incisions all the way along each edge of the feather shape. Cut from the outer edge of the feather towards the centre, repeating the process on both sides.

3 Punch a small hole at each end of the feather shape and attach a jump ring through each hole.

4 Paint a thin line of fabric paint along the centre on the front of the feather to create its spine.

5 Take some beading wire and thread it through one of the jump rings until the jump ring is halfway along the beading wire. Place the ends of the beading wire together and thread on half the strand of beads.

6 Thread a crimp onto both pieces of beading wire, then attach a toggle clasp to one end and the toggle bar to the other end. Tuck the end of the beading wire back through the crimp. Press the crimp together tightly with a pair of flat-nosed pliers.

7 Trim the excess beading wire with the cutters. Attach a crimp cover over the crimp. Repeat this process on the other end of the necklace.

8 To make the earrings, repeat steps 1 to 4, using the excess leather from the necklace. Make the feather shapes a quarter of the size of the necklace feather. Attach a second jump ring and then an earring wire to the jump ring for each earring.

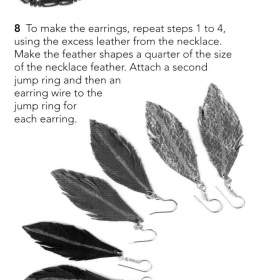

Choose the beads you prefer to make this necklace. You can use one type only, or mix and match to make it uniquely yours.

Stamped Pendant

Materials:

Sheet of card

7 x 9cm (2¾ x 3½in) piece of vegetable tan leather

1 x 9mm (³/₈in) gold-coloured jump ring

2 x 6mm (¼in) jump rings

1 x 5mm (¼in) gold-coloured head pin

1m (39½in) length of gold-coloured chain

1 x gold-coloured clasp

Fabric paint or leather dye in the colours of your choice

Gold or bronze mica powder

1 x 10mm (½in) bead

Tools:

Ballpoint pen

Leather shears

Rotary hole punch

Round-nosed pliers

2 x flat-nosed pliers

Decorative stamping tools (camouflage and veiner designs)

Polymer mallet

Paintbrush

Bone folder

Cotton rag

Paper towel

Instructions:

1 Draw a leaf shape measuring approximately 5 x 8cm (2 x 3¼in) onto a piece of card and cut it out to use as a template. Draw around the card template onto the leather and cut it out.

2 Wet the leather with some warm water until it is slightly damp on the front and back, but do not saturate it. Pat the surface dry with a paper towel. Take a spare piece of leather, wet this and practise applying a pattern with the decorative stamp on this first.

3 Take a decorative stamping tool and position the base of the tool onto the smooth side of the leather. Strike the top of the stamp with a polymer mallet to make an impression onto the leather. Repeat the process to create the desired pattern on your leather pendant.

4 Mould the leather pendant so that it has curved edges and allow it to dry out. After it has dried, moisten the edges with a damp cotton rag. Rub the rag vigorously along the edges to smooth the leather. Rub the bone folder along the edges until they are smooth.

5 Paint the front of the pendant with fabric paint or leather dye. After drying, apply some gold or bronze mica powder to the surface of the pendant.

6 Punch a hole at the top and bottom of the pendant with the rotary tool. Thread a head pin through a bead and turn the head pin to a 45-degree angle with a pair of flat-nosed pliers. Use round-nosed pliers to turn a loop in the head pin at the top of the bead. Attach this to the hole at the base of the pendant. Wrap the excess wire around the top of the bead.

7 Attach a 9mm (³/₈in) jump ring to the hole at the top of the pendant. Thread the gold chain through the jump ring. Attach a 6mm (¼in) jump ring and clasp to each end of the chain.

Roses Necklace & Ring Set

Materials:

Sheet of card

15 x 15cm (6 x 6in) piece of orange nappa leather

Leather glue

3 x 5cm (2in) silver eye pins

40cm (15¾in) strand of clear quartz 8mm (⁵/₁₆in) beads

Silver-coloured clasp

4 x crimps and crimp covers

1.5m (59in) length of beading wire

1 x adjustable ring with blank bezel

Tools:

Ballpoint pen

Leather scissors

2 x flat-nosed pliers

Round-nosed pliers

Wire cutters

Instructions:

1 Draw a heart shape measuring 3 x 3cm (1¼ x 1¼in) and another measuring 2 x 2cm (¾ x ¾in) onto a piece of card and cut these out. Draw around the templates on the nappa leather with a ballpoint pen. Cut out two of the smaller hearts and three of the larger hearts for each leather rose. Make sure that you cut them out inside the ballpoint pen outline so that this does not show.

2 Apply some glue halfway up one of the small hearts. You can choose to have the suede or smooth side of the leather facing outwards, or use a combination of both. Place an eye pin lengthways down the centre of the heart. Take one edge of the heart and roll it up tightly.

3 Apply some leather glue to another small heart. Stick this around the heart you curled up previously.

4 Apply some glue to one of the larger hearts and stick this on top of the previous heart. Fold back the curved part of the heart so that it begins to form a rose petal shape. Repeat this process with the other two large heart shapes.

5 Form another two roses using the hearts and allow the glue to dry.

6 Trim the end of the eye pin with wire cutters, leaving 1cm (½in) of wire above the rose. Use the round-nosed pliers to bend the wire to a 45-degree angle. Form a loop with the round-nosed pliers. Repeat this process with each rose.

7 Open the eye pins and attach them to one another so the roses are connected. Thread some beading wire through the last eye pin on the right. Thread a crimp through both ends of the beading wire. Use flat-nosed pliers to flatten the crimp. Place a crimp cover over the crimp. Thread on the beads until you have the desired necklace length. Repeat this process on the other side of the necklace.

8 Attach a crimp, crimp cover and a clasp at each end of the necklace.

9 To make the ring, use the excess leather to create another rose shape but do not insert an eye pin into the centre. Trim the leather at the base of the rose so that it is flat. Apply some glue to the blank bezel inside the ring. Press the base of the rose firmly into the glue and allow the glue to dry for two hours.

Bib-style Flower Necklace

Materials:

Sheet of card

3 x pieces of nappa leather measuring 30 x 30cm (11¾ x 11¾in) in fuchsia pink, red and brown

Leather glue

4 x 5cm (2in) head pins

2 x 9mm ($^3/_8$in) jump rings

50cm (19¾in) length of gold-coloured chain

2 x 6mm (¼in) gold-coloured jump rings

1 x gold-coloured clasp

4 x 8mm ($^5/_{16}$in) faceted round clear quartz beads

Tools:

Ballpoint pen

Leather scissors

Bowl of hand-hot water

Paper towel

Non-stick baking liner

Baking tray

Rotary hole punch

Awl

Round-nosed pliers

2 x flat-nosed pliers

Wire cutters

Instructions:

1 Draw four different flower shapes onto a piece of card with the following diameters: 10cm (4in), 7cm (2¾in), 5cm (2in) and 3.5cm (1$^3/_8$in). Cut these shapes out to use as templates.

2 Draw around the largest flower template on the fuchsia pink and the red leather and cut them out.

3 Repeat this process, cutting out one small flower in fuchsia pink and red, and two each of the two middle sizes in fuchsia pink and red. You will have twelve flowers in total.

4 Place all the leather flower shapes into a bowl of hand-hot water. Remove them and squeeze any excess water out of the leather shapes. Pat the shapes dry with a paper towel.

5 Fold each flower in half, and then in half again to form a v-shape. Roll the wet leather up tightly lengthways. Repeat this process with each flower shape. Place the flowers onto a baking tray lined with a sheet of non-stick baking liner. Bake at 60°C/140°F/gas mark ¼ for 15 minutes or until the flowers have dried.

6 When they are dry, open up the flower shapes. Assemble them into four complete

flowers – using three shapes per flower – placing the shapes on top of one another in descending order, with the largest shape at the bottom. Glue the shapes together.

7 Make a hole with an awl in the centre of each flower. Thread a quartz bead onto a head pin, then push the end of the head pin through the hole in the centre of the flower. Use the round-nosed pliers to create a loop with the head pin wire at the back of the flower. Wrap the excess wire around the base of the loop. Bend the loop back so it lies flat against the back of the flower. Repeat this process with each flower.

8 To create the bib necklace base, draw a crescent shape onto a piece of card measuring 5 x 14cm (2 x 5½in). Cut this shape out and draw around it on the brown leather. Cut the leather shape out.

9 Place the brown leather suede side up and apply glue all around the edges. Fold the edges of the leather inwards by 5mm (¼in) and stick it down all the way around the edge.

10 Position the flowers on the right side of the bib. Apply some glue to the back of each flower and stick them onto the bib.

11 Use a rotary punch to cut a hole at each end of the bib, then attach a 9mm (³/₈in) jump ring through the hole using flat-nosed pliers. Cut the chain into two equal lengths using wire cutters. Attach one end of the chain to the jump ring and attach a 6mm (¼in) jump ring to the other end of the chain. Repeat this process on the other side and attach a clasp to the 6mm (¼in) jump rings.

Soutache-style Set

Materials:

Pendant: 1 x flat-back cabochon stone approx. 3cm (1¼in) in diameter

5 x strips of leather in different colours measuring 1.5 x 18cm (½ x 7in)

6 x 6cm (2¼ x 2¼in) piece of nappa leather

Leather glue

15cm (6in) length of copper-coloured wire (0.8 gauge)

3 x 1m (39½in) lengths of leather cord in different colours

Copper-coloured cord ends with clasp

Earrings: 2 x flat-back cabochon stone approx. 2cm (¾in) in diameter

5 x strips of leather in different colours measuring 1.5 x 18cm (½ x 7in)

2 x 6cm (2¼in) lengths of copper-coloured wire (0.8 gauge)

4 x square copper spacer beads

6 x 6mm (¼in) copper-coloured jump rings

2 x copper-coloured earwires

Tools:

Leather scissors

Bone folder

Awl

Round-nosed pliers

2 x flat-nosed pliers

Instructions:

1 Apply some glue along the long edge of each leather strip. Fold the strips of leather in half lengthways and crease together with the bone folder.

2 Apply some glue to the back of the cabochon and place it in the centre of the square piece of leather, suede side up.

3 Apply some glue about the cabochon and onto the leather square. Wrap one of the strips of leather around the edge of the cabochon. Wrap the remaining strips of leather around one another to form the pendant.

4 Trim the excess leather from the base of the pendant with leather scissors.

5 Make a large hole with an awl through the leather above the top of the cabochon and push the copper wire through it. Use round-nosed pliers to form a loop at the top of the pendant. Push the wire through the hole twice more to form three loops. Wrap the excess wire around the base of the loops and form two spirals with the ends of the wire.

6 Braid the three lengths of leather cord and attach cord ends to each end. Thread the cord through the wire loops at the top of the pendant.

7 To make the earrings follow the process in steps 1 to 4. Make a large hole with an awl through the leather above the top of the cabochon.

8 Take a 6cm (2¼in) length of copper wire and thread it through the hole in the leather. Thread a spacer bead onto the wire at the front of the earring. Bend both pieces of wire upwards to meet one another.

9 Bend the wires to a 90-degree angle then bend them over a pair of round-nosed pliers to create a loop. Attach a second spacer bead so that it sits inside the wire loop. Wrap the excess wire around the base of the second spacer bead.

10 Repeat the process in step 9 but instead of adding a spacer bead to the loop, attach a jump ring. Use flat-nosed pliers to attach two more jump rings. Attach an earwire to the last jump ring.

11 Repeat the process in steps 7 to 10 to complete the second earring.

'Soutache' means a 'flat, ornamental braid' and here the coloured leather strips are used to decorate the edges of the beautiful cabochon stones.

Lariat Tassel Necklace

Materials:

1m (39½in) plaited leather cord

20 x 20cm (7¾ x 7¾in) piece of
  nappa leather

Leather glue

Tools:

Leather scissors

Wire cutters

Instructions:

1 Cut a long triangular strip of leather
measuring 20cm (7¾in) long. The base of the
strip should measure 2.5cm (1in) and taper to a
point at the top.

2 Apply a layer of glue to the suede side of the
leather. Fold the plaited leather cord in half.
Place the wide end of the triangular strip of
leather glue side down and begin to wrap the
leather strip around both pieces of cord 10cm
(4in) from the bottom.

3 Cut two strips of nappa leather measuring
5 x 8cm (2 x 3¼in). Cut a fringe along the long
edge of both strips of leather. Leave a 1cm
(½in) margin at the top of each piece.

4 Apply a layer of glue along the margin on
the long edge of each strip. Wrap the strip
tightly around the bottom of each end of the
plaited cord.

*Multicoloured, metallic
braided leather is very widely
available and here it looks
striking against a black outfit.*

Ruff-style Necklace & Cuff

Materials:

30 x 45cm (11¾ x 17¾in) piece of pink nappa leather

Leather glue

2 x clasps

4 x 9mm (³/₈in) jump rings

1m (39½in) suede cord

Strand of 8mm (⁵/₁₆in) pearls

1m (39½in) length of beading wire

4 x crimps and crimp covers

12cm (4¾in) length of chain

Tools:

Leather scissors

Rotary hole punch

2 x flat-nosed pliers

Instructions:

1 Cut a piece of leather measuring 20 x 30cm (7¾ x 11¾in). Apply a 2.5cm (1in) line of glue lengthways along the centre of the piece of nappa leather.

2 Fold the top and bottom long edges of the leather inwards so that they meet in the middle and stick them down.

3 Allow the glue to dry. Make incisions along the long edge on both sides of the leather. Leave a 2.5cm (1in) wide gap in the middle of the leather.

4 Punch a hole through the middle of the leather on both of the short edges. Attach a jump ring through each hole with the flat-nosed pliers.

5 Thread a strand of pearls onto some beading wire. Place a crimp onto the beading wire at one end of the pearl strand. Feed the wire back through the crimp to form a 1cm (½in) loop and press the crimp down with the flat-nosed pliers. Attach a crimp cover. Repeat the process at the other end.

6 Open the jump ring with the flat-nosed pliers and attach the pearls to the jump ring with the bead wire loop. Attach a 6cm (2¼in) length of chain to the jump ring. Attach a clasp to the other end of the chain. Repeat the process on the other side of the necklace.

7 To make the cuff, cut a piece of leather measuring 14 x 21cm (5½ x 8¼in). Apply a 2.5cm (1in) line of glue lengthways along the centre of the leather.

8 Then follow the process in steps 2–4.

9 Apply a thin line of glue along the centre of the leather on the front of the cuff. Cut the

suede cord in half and stick the two lengths of cord to the glue. Trim the ends of the cord so that they are flush with the ends of the cuff.

10 Open a jump ring with the flat-nosed pliers and attach to the hole at one end of the cuff. Attach the clasp to the jump ring and close it. Repeat this process at the other end of the cuff to attach the second jump ring and toggle bar.

Pompom Ring

Materials:

18 x 8cm (7 x 3¼in) piece of
    nappa or pig suede leather
1 x 10mm (½in) clear
    quartz bead
Leather glue
1 x ring blank
1 x 5cm (2in) head pin

Tools:

Paintbrush
Leather scissors
Wire cutters

Instructions:

1 Use a paintbrush to apply a line of glue
to one side of the long edges of the nappa
leather. Fold the other long edge up, stick the
two edges together and leave to dry.

2 Use some leather scissors to cut a fringe into
the folded leather. Leave a 1cm (½in) margin at
the glued edge.

3 Apply some glue to the long edge of the
leather fringe. Thread a bead onto a head pin.
Place the excess wire of the head pin onto

the edge of the leather and begin to roll the
leather up tightly to create a pompom. Make
sure the head pin and bead are sitting snugly
within the centre of the rolled-up leather.

4 Trim off the excess wire from the head pin at
the base of the pompom shape.

5 Apply some glue to the base of the pompom
and inside the ring blank. Place the pompom
into the ring blank and allow to dry.

*This ring is sure to make an impact.
Go for a central bead colour that
complements the leather and choose
a silver- or gold-coloured ring blank to
match the rest of your jewellery.*

Wire-wrapped Flower Ring

Materials:

Piece of card

10 x 10cm (4 x 4in) piece of nappa leather

1 x 8mm (⁵/₁₆in) bead

0.5m (19¾in) length of beading wire (0.8mm gauge)

Tools:

Ballpoint pen

Leather scissors

Bowl of hand-hot water

Ring mandrel

Awl

Wire cutters

Instructions:

1 Draw a flower shape measuring 2.5cm (1in) in diameter onto a piece of card. Mine has eight petals. Cut the shape out.

2 Place the card flower template on the leather, draw around it with the ballpoint pen and cut out the leather flower. Repeat this process so that you have two leather flowers.

3 Soak the flowers in hand-hot water. Dry off the excess water with a paper towel, then scrunch up the flowers and leave them to dry.

4 Put the two leather flower shapes together, one on top of the other, and pierce a hole through the centre of them with the awl.

5 Thread a bead onto the middle of the length of wire and press the wires together so that they meet underneath the bead. Twist to secure the bead.

6 Thread both strands of wire through the hole in the centre of the flowers. Wrap the excess wire around the place on the ring mandrel that corresponds with your finger size.

7 Wrap each strand of wire around the mandrel twice. Take the excess of one strand of wire around the four coils of wire and wrap it underneath the leather flower. Repeat this process with the other strand of wire and trim off the excess.

Nappa leather is available in a wide range of colours, so you could make several of these rings to go with different outfits.

Painted Cuff

Materials:

3 x 20cm (1¼ x 7⁷/₈in) piece of vegetable tan leather

Leather glue

Small diamanté buckle

1m (39½in) length of silver suede cord

Silver fabric paint

1 x large snap fastener

2.5 x 19.5cm (1 x 7¾in) piece of nappa or pig suede leather

Tools:

Leather scissors

Rotary hole punch

Paintbrush

Cotton rag

Bone folder

Instructions:

1 Rub the edges of the piece of vegetable tan leather vigorously with a damp cotton rag. Then rub the edges with a bone folder until they feel smooth.

2 Paint the front and sides of the leather with silver fabric paint. The leather may need two or three coats of paint. Allow the paint to dry between coats.

3 Cut the leather cord into six equal lengths and thread them through the diamanté buckle. Apply a layer of glue along the back of the cords and stick them along the middle of the

leather lengthways. Trim any excess leather cord at the ends of the bracelet with the leather scissors.

4 Take the piece of nappa or pig suede leather and apply glue to the inside of the bracelet and stick the leather onto it, with the suede side facing outwards.

5 Once it has dried, punch a hole at each end of the bracelet and attach the snap fastener.

Use the same techniques to create different designs. In the main picture the leather for the top cuff has been painted black, and pearls and gemstones have been added with wire (see page 28 for details about this technique).

Wet-formed Cuff

Materials:

4.5 x 18cm (1¾ x 7in) piece of vegetable tan leather

Leather dye in the colour of your choice

Gold and bronze fabric paint

1m (39½in) length of beading wire (0.6mm gauge)

Assorted beads

Tools:

Paintbrush

Bowl of hand-hot water

Paper towel

Non-stick baking liner

Baking tray

Sponge

Awl

Instructions:

1 Saturate the piece of leather in some hand-hot water, then pat it dry with a paper towel. Place the leather into a preheated very cool oven on 80°C/176°F/gas mark ¼ on a baking tray with a non-stick baking liner. Heat for 10 minutes.

2 Remove the warm leather from the oven and sculpt and mould it into a cuff shape. Place it back in the oven for a further 10 minutes or until the leather is dry.

3 Allow the leather to cool, then paint some leather dye onto the back and front of the cuff. You may need to apply two or three coats of dye. Let it dry in between coats.

4 Using a piece of sponge, apply some gold and bronze fabric paint to the front of the cuff. Use a stippling motion with the sponge so that the paint appears mottled.

5 Allow the paint to dry. Use an awl to pierce two holes through the centre of the cuff. Thread a bead onto a piece of wire, bend the wire over the bead and twist three times. Repeat this process by adding more beads to the wire until you have a cluster of beads.

6 Push the excess wire through the first hole in the cuff until the bead cluster is flush with the leather. Push the wire back through the second hole and wrap the excess wire around the bead cluster.

7 You can paint the inside of the cuff to make it feel smoother against the skin. You may also like to use a small offcut of fashion leather to line the cuff. Cut a piece of fashion leather 2.5cm (1in) smaller than your cuff all the way around. Apply some glue to the shiny side of the fashion leather (so that the suede side will be facing outwards) and stick it to the inside of the cuff.

Cuff with Natural Polish

Materials:

4.5 x 18cm (1¾ x 7in) piece of vegetable tan leather

Natural leather polish

4 x 17.5cm (1½ x 6³/₈in) piece of nappa leather

1m (39½in) length of beading wire (0.6mm gauge)

7 beads ranging in size from 4–8mm (³/₁₆–⁵/₁₆in)

Tools:

Leather scissors

Bowl of hand-hot water

Paper towel

Non-stick baking liner

Baking tray

Cotton rag

Awl

Instructions:

1 Saturate the piece of leather in some hand-hot water, then pat it dry with a paper towel. Place the leather into a preheated very cool oven on 80°C/176°F/gas mark ¼ on a baking tray with a non-stick baking liner. Heat for 10 minutes.

2 Remove the warm leather from the oven and sculpt and mould it into a cuff shape. Place it back in the oven for a further 10 minutes or until the leather is dry.

3 Allow the leather to cool. Apply some natural leather polish onto the front of the leather using a cotton rag. Buff the leather with a clean piece of cotton rag to help the polish sink into the leather and to give it polished, shiny surface.

4 Using an awl, pierce seven holes at equal intervals along the middle of the cuff. Thread a bead onto a piece of wire, bend the wire over the bead and twist the wire. Push the wire through the first hole. Feed the wire along the back of the cuff and up through the second hole. Add another bead and repeat this process until all seven beads are attached to the leather.

5 Push the excess wire flat against the back of the cuff. Apply some glue to the back of the cuff and stick the nappa leather to this, with the suede side facing outwards.

Bead Bracelet

Materials:

30 x 30cm (11¾ x 11¾in) piece of nappa leather

1m (39½in) length of wire (1mm gauge)

Bracelet clasp

Leather glue

Tools:

Leather scissors

Round-nosed pliers

Wire cutters

Instructions:

1 Cut a strip of nappa leather measuring 3 x 4cm (1¼ x 1½in) to create the tassel. Cut a fringe along the long edge leaving a 1cm (½in) margin at the top.

2 Apply a layer of glue along the margin on the long edge. Place a 6cm (2¼in) length of wire at one end of the short edge and wrap the strip tightly around the wire. Form a loop with the excess wire at the top of the tassel with round-nosed pliers. Wrap the excess wire around the base of the loop.

3 Cut six long triangular strips of leather measuring 20cm (7¾in). The base of the strip should measure 2.5cm (1in) and taper to a point at the top.

4 Apply a layer of glue to the suede side of the leather. Cut off a 6cm (2¼in) length of wire and place this on top of the glued leather strip at the wide end.

5 Begin to roll the leather strip around the piece of wire tightly to form a bead shape. Repeat the process in steps 3 and 4 to create another five beads and allow the glue to dry.

6 Trim the wire so that there is just 1cm (½in) protruding from both ends of each bead and form a loop at the end using the round-nosed pliers.

7 Connect all the beads to one another by opening a wire loop, linking the next bead and closing the loop.

8 Attach the clasp to the final loop at either end of the bracelet, then attach the tassel to one of the loops at the end.

Fashion Flower Cuff

Materials:

Piece of card

2 x pieces of 30 x 30cm (11¾ x 11¾in) nappa leather in coordinating colours

2 x 4mm (³/₁₆in) Sam Browne studs

5 x 4mm (³/₁₆in) pearls

5 x 5cm (2in) head pins

Leather glue

Tools:

Ballpoint pen

Leather scissors

Bowl of hand-hot water

Paper towel

Baking tray

Non-stick baking liner

Bone folder

Rotary hole punch

Awl

Instructions:

1 Cut out a piece of leather measuring 8 x 23cm (3¼ x 9in). Apply some glue 1cm (½in) in along each edge of the suede side.

2 Fold over a 1.5cm (½in) hem of leather all the way round and stick down. Use a bone folder to crease the folded edges of the leather and make them flat.

3 Draw five flower shapes on the card: two with a 10cm (4in) diameter, one with a 7cm (2¾in) diameter and two with a 5cm (2in) diameter. Draw around these templates on the second piece of leather and cut them out.

4 Place each leather flower shape in a bowl of hand-hot water. Remove them and squeeze out the excess water, then pat the flowers dry with a paper towel.

5 Fold each flower in half, and then in half again to form a v-shape. Roll the wet leather up tightly lengthways. Place the flowers in a

preheated oven on a baking tray lined with a non-stick baking liner. Bake for 15 minutes at 60°C/140°F/gas mark ¼ or until the flowers have dried.

6 Remove from the oven and allow to cool. Assemble the leather shapes into a complete flower by placing them on top of one another in descending order, with the largest shape first. Some can be leather side up and some suede side up. Apply leather glue to the underside of each flower to keep them in place.

7 When the glue is dry, pierce a hole through the centre of the flowers with an awl. Thread each pearl onto a head pin, and push the ends of the head pins through the hole in the flower. Twist the excess wires together and bend them flat against the back of the leather.

8 Cut a piece of leather measuring 6 x 18cm (2¼ x 7in) in a coordinating colour. Apply some glue all over the shiny side of the leather. Stick this to the back of the cuff to cover the head pin wires and create a soft, suede lining for the cuff.

9 Punch a hole in the middle of one of the short edges of the cuff with a rotary hole punch. Screw a Sam Browne stud through the hole. Punch a corresponding hole at the opposite end of the cuff, ensuring it is big enough for the stud to fit through.

Pearl and Gem Cuff

Materials:

30 x 30cm (11¾ x 11¾in) piece of red or orange
nappa leather

3 x 4mm (³/₁₆ in) Sam Browne studs

Approx. 20 x 8mm (⁵/₁₆in) pearls or clear quartz beads

50cm (19¾in) length of beading wire (0.6mm gauge)

Leather glue

Tools:

Leather scissors

Bone folder

Rotary hole punch

Awl

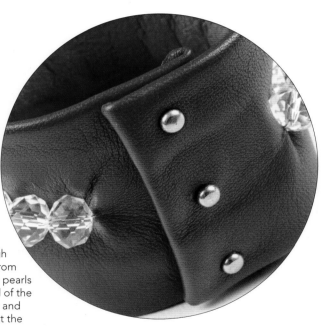

Instructions:

1 Cut out a piece of leather
measuring 8 x 25cm (3¼ x 9¾in).
Apply some glue 1cm (½in) in from
the edge all round on the suede
side of the leather.

2 Fold over a 1.5cm (½in) hem
of leather all the way around and
stick it down. Use a bone folder to
crease the edges of the leather and
make them flat.

3 Using an awl, pierce a hole through
each end of the leather 3cm (1¼in) from
the short edge. Thread the beads or pearls
onto a length of wire. Push each end of the
wire through the holes in the leather and
bend the ends of the wire flat against the
back of the leather.

4 Cut another piece of leather measuring 4.5 x
19.5cm (1¾ x 7¾in). Apply some glue all over the
shiny side of the leather. Stick this to the back of
the cuff to cover the wire and create a soft, suede
lining for the cuff.

5 Punch three holes along one of the short
edges of the cuff with the rotary hole punch.
Screw Sam Browne studs through the holes.
Punch three corresponding holes on of the
opposite end of the cuff, ensuring that they
are big enough for the studs to fit through.

36

Cord and Chain Earrings

Materials:

32cm (12½in) leather cord

38cm (15in) length of chain

2 x cord ends

2 x s-shaped clasps

2 x fish hook earwires

8 x 5mm (¼in) jump rings

8 x 4mm (³/₁₆in) pearls

8 x 5cm (2in) head pins

Tools:

Leather scissors

Wire cutters

Round-nosed pliers

2 x flat-nosed pliers

Instructions:

1 Cut four 4cm (1½in) lengths of leather cord. Attach a cord end to the top of all the pieces of cord with the flat-nosed pliers.

2 Cut four pieces of chain to varying lengths using wire cutters. Thread a pearl onto a head pin and attach the head pin and pearl to the bottom of a piece of chain by making a wrapped loop with round-nosed pliers. Repeat this process for each of the pieces of chain. Add additional pearls halfway up each piece of chain.

3 Attach a jump ring to the top of each piece of chain with flat-nosed pliers. Place the jump rings and cord ends onto one end of the s-shaped clasp.

4 Attach an earwire to the other end of the s-shaped clasp with flat-nosed pliers. Repeat the process for the second earring.

Plaited Cord Earrings

Materials:

1 x 20cm (7¾in) length of white
  plaited leather cord

4 x cord ends

4 x 6mm (¼in) jump rings

2 x fish hook earwires

2 x 5cm (2in) head pins

2 x 6mm (¼in) green beads

Tools:

Leather scissors

Round-nosed pliers

2 x flat-nosed pliers

Instructions:

1 Thread a bead onto a head pin. Form a
loop with the wire at the top of the bead using
round-nosed pliers. Wrap the excess wire
around the base of the loop.

2 Cut a 10cm (4in) length of plaited leather
cord. Thread the cord through the wire loop.

3 Attach cord ends to each end of the leather
cord using flat-nosed pliers. Attach a jump
ring to connect the two ends of the leather
cord together.

4 Attach another jump ring to the first jump
ring, then attach the earwire. Repeat the
process for the second earring.

*These earrings are a great project
to experiment with. Try some
combinations where the bead
colour complements the leather,
and also some contrasting colours
to achieve different effects.*

Calla Lily Earrings

Materials:

Piece of card

15 x 15cm (6 x 6in) piece of gold nappa leather

Leather glue

2 x 6mm (¼in) beads

22cm (8¾in) length of wire (0.6 gauge)

2 x fish hook earwires

Tools:

Leather scissors

Round-nosed pliers

2 x flat-nosed pliers

Wire cutters

Instructions:

1 Draw a petal shape onto a piece of card measuring 3 x 4cm (1¼ x 1½in). Cut this out to use as a template. Draw around the template onto the leather and cut out two petal shapes.

2 Cut two lengths of wire with wire cutters, one measuring 6cm (2¼in) long and the other measuring 5cm (2in).

3 Thread a bead onto each of the lengths of wire and coil the end of the wire twice with the round-nosed pliers.

4 Place the two pieces of wire on top of a leather petal shape with the pointed end of the petal at the top. Position the wires so that the

beads are slightly lower than the base of the petal and so that the top of the wires are aligned.

5 Apply a little glue to the top of the petal and roll the ends together to form the calla lily shape. Form a loop with the two excess pieces of wire and wrap the excess wire around the base of the loop and around the top of the leather. Attach an earwire to the loop.

6 Repeat the process for the second earring.

Flower Cufflinks

Materials:

4 x 10cm (1½ x 4in) piece of nappa
   or pig suede leather

Leather glue

T-bar clasp

3cm (1¼in) length of chain

2 x 6mm (¼in) beads

2 x 5cm (2in) head pins

Tools:

Leather scissors

2 x flat-nosed pliers

Round-nosed pliers

2 x 5mm (¼in) jump rings

Instructions:

1 Cut a piece of leather measuring 2 x 10cm
(¾ x 4in). Apply a line of glue to one side of the
long edge. Fold the other edge up, stick both
edges together and allow to dry.

2 Cut a fringe into the folded leather with
the leather scissors. Leave a 5mm (¼in)
margin at the top of the leather. Cut the
leather in half widthways.

3 Apply some glue to the long edge of the
leather fringe. Thread a bead onto a head pin.
Place the excess wire of the head pin onto the
edge of the leather and begin to roll the leather
up tightly. Make sure the head pin and bead are
sitting snugly within the centre of the rolled up
leather. Repeat this to make a second cufflink.

4 Bend the excess wire from the head pin to a
45-degree angle. Grip the wire with the round-
nosed pliers and create a loop.

5 Place a piece of chain measuring 1.5cm (½in)
inside the loop. Wrap the excess wire around
the base of the loop.

6 Attach a jump ring to the end of the chain
with flat-nosed pliers and attach a T-bar clasp to
the jump ring.

7 Repeat steps 4, 5 and 6 to complete the
second cufflink.

Fob Pendant

Materials:

3 x 8.5cm (1¼ x 3³/₈ in)
piece of nappa leather

Leather glue

47.5cm (18¾in) length of
waxed cord

1 x 8cm (3¼in) length of
beading wire (0.8 gauge)

Tools:

Leather scissors

Awl

Round-nosed pliers

Wire cutters

Instructions:

1 Cut the length of wire with the wire cutters
and then form the wire into a tight coil with the
round-nosed pliers. Leave a 2cm (¾in) length of
wire at the top of the coil.

2 Make a hole through the piece of leather
with an awl, 2cm (¾in) from the bottom of the
leather lengthways.

3 Push the excess wire through the hole so that
the coil is flush with the leather, then bend the
excess wire so that it is flat with the back of the
leather piece.

4 Apply some glue to the back of the leather,
but only to the first 1.5cm (½in) from the top.

5 Fold the top of the leather over and stick it to
the back of the pendant.

6 Thread the waxed cord through the gap
where the leather is folded. Knot the waxed
cord to tie around the neckline, or attach cord
endings and a clasp if preferred.

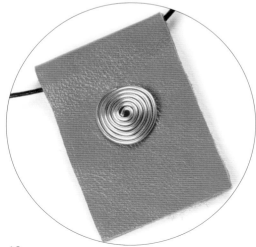

*This unisex pendant is quick and
easy to make and has a stylish
simplicity – just choose a colour
to suit the wearer.*

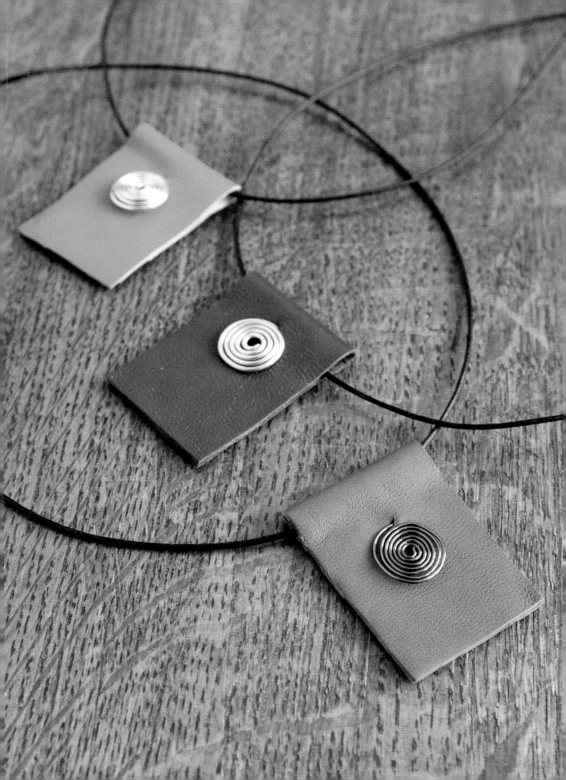

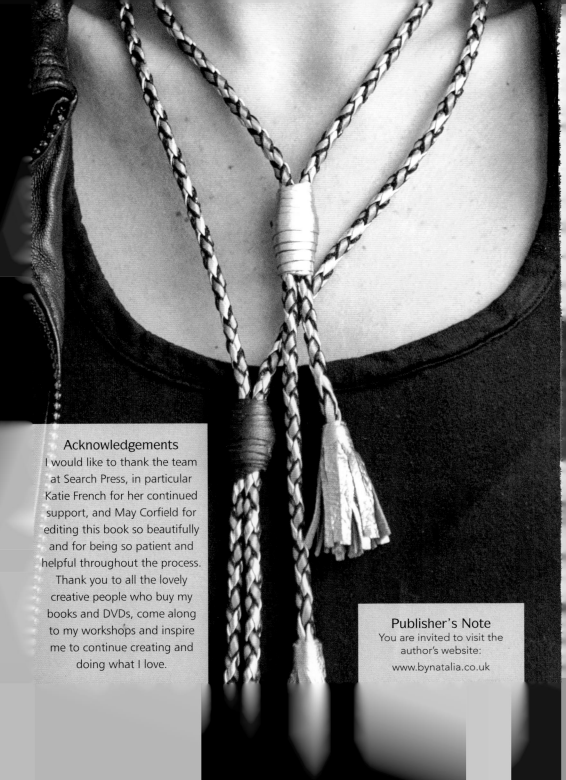

Acknowledgements

I would like to thank the team at Search Press, in particular Katie French for her continued support, and May Corfield for editing this book so beautifully and for being so patient and helpful throughout the process.

Thank you to all the lovely creative people who buy my books and DVDs, come along to my workshops and inspire me to continue creating and doing what I love.

Publisher's Note

You are invited to visit the author's website:

www.bynatalia.co.uk